Financial Healing from the Inside Out

Angela C. Preston
Dr. Amanda H. Goodson

Financial Healing from the Inside Out
by Angela C. Preston and
Dr. Amanda H. Goodson

© **2019 by** Angela C. Preston and
Amanda H. Goodson
All rights reserved.

Edited by Adam Colwell's WriteWorks, LLC: Adam Colwell and Ginger Colwell
Cover Design by Terrell Payton
Typesetting by Gretchen Dorris, Ink to Book
Published by Goodson Publishing

Printed in the United States of America

All rights reserved. Except in the case of brief quotations embodied in critical articles and reviews, no portion of this book may be reproduced, stored in a retrieval system, or transmitted in any form or by any means—electronic, mechanical, photocopy, recording, scanning, or other—without the prior written permission from the author. None of the material in this book may be reproduced for any commercial promotion, advertising or sale of a product or service.

Scripture quotations marked (KJV) are from the KING JAMES VERSION, public domain.

Scripture quotations marked (NKJV) are taken from the NEW KING JAMES VER-SION®. Copyright© 1982 by Thomas Nelson, Inc. Used by permission. All rights reserved.

Scripture quotations marked (ESV) are taken from THE HOLY BIBLE, ENGLISH STANDARD VERSION®, Copyright© 2001 by Crossway, a publishing ministry of Good News Publishers. Used by permission.

Scripture quotations marked (NIV) are taken from THE HOLY BIBLE, NEW INTERNATIONAL VERSION®. Copyright© 1973, 1978, 1984, 2011 by Biblica, Inc.™. Used by permission of Zondervan.

Scripture quotations marked (NASB) are taken from the NEW AMERICAN STANDARD BIBLE®, Copyright© 1960, 1962, 1963, 1968, 1971, 1972, 1973, 1975, 1977, 1995 by The Lockman Foundation. Used by permission.

Scripture quotations marked (ASV) are taken from the American Standard Version Bible (Public Domain).

Dedications

Angela:

Thank you to my husband, Otis, for your unwavering love and support. Thank you for the encouragement when I was pressed to meet deadlines and felt overwhelmed, and for all you do to support my visions and my dreams! Love you, Always & Forever! To my son, Calvin. You challenged my thinking, always presented a fresh perspective, and have shown how much you love and support me. Thank you. I love you.

To my mom, Charlotte. Your love is unfailing as you have prayed, spoken the Word over me and to me, and journeyed and labored with me. No words can express how much I love you!

To my extended family, thank you for your support, encouragement, and all that you do to enable me to focus on my work. I love you.

Amanda:

I dedicate this book to my husband, Lonnie. You are so patient with me as I have all these wonderful ideas to speak, coach, educate, and help people grow to a better place, both strategically and personally, professionally. Your calm and steady support is phenomenal—and I love you deeply for that. To my son, Jelonni, who brings light and hope to so many people. Thank you for understanding your mom and loving me like I am. I respect the person you are becoming and honor the fact that you're pursuing your dreams! Mom, Beth, and Princetta, thank you for everything! I cannot express how much I appreciate your support for all my efforts and your love for me throughout them.

Table of Contents

PREFACE ix
The Heart of Your Finances

CHAPTER ONE 1
Your First Investment

CHAPTER TWO 15
Rebellion and Control

CHAPTER THREE 33
Gaining a Wealthy Mindset

CHAPTER FOUR 47
Reviving Your Financial Future

CHAPTER FIVE 65
Dreaming and Thinking Your Way to Financial Freedom

ABOUT THE AUTHORS 91

Preface

The Heart of Your Finances

Do you want to know how to be more creative with your financial capital? Are you like the millions of Americans who desire to leverage their capital to create wealth for generations to come? In this book, we will use biblical principles to explore wealth creation and help you to develop a more healthy perspective about money that will lead to your financial healing.

In a typical year, more than 40 million Americans will suffer from some type of debilitating anxiety. This leads me to believe that anxiety exists in epidemic proportions in our culture—and is what robs us of our peace.

As we look at anxiety from a financial perspective, it usually comes in the form of stress that keeps you up a night. Generally, this isn't the result of not being able to eat out as often or not having extra money for shopping. This level of debilitating anxiety occurs when we feel as if we do not have enough money to pay our bills, to participate in leisure activities, to acquire certain assets, and to accomplish our goals or fulfill our destiny.

When we believe we're running out of money, or we don't have enough money to take care of necessities, we become anxious because money is not flowing as freely as it should.

This is the type of financial stress that transforms into distress—where our stress levels begin to block our ability to think rationally and make wise financial decisions concerning our current and future earnings. At this stage, we must ask ourselves, "How am I allowing myself to be robbed of my peace when it comes to my financial stability?" "How did I get trapped into financial barriers that are keeping me psychologically bound and physically drained?"

"Be anxious for nothing, but in everything by prayer and supplication, with thanksgiving, let your requests be made known to God; and the peace of God, which surpasses all understanding, will guard your hearts and minds through Christ Jesus."

Philippians 4:6-7, NKJV

Jesus instructed His disciples to be anxious for nothing; in other words, to not worry about anything. Anxiousness will not get you to a place of healing when it comes to how you see your finances. But if you can remove yourself from the confines of stress and worry and begin traveling a road to financial healing, your mindset will be propelled into proper channels of wellness to freely receive the peace God has available for you.

Being anxious for nothing requires you to not be concerned, afraid, nervous, hesitant, or reserved. Do not allow yourself to become so consumed with anything that you place yourself in the position of forfeiting your peace. God wants to restore it, but the process will take discipline, faith, and work.

THE HEART OF YOUR FINANCES: EMOTIONAL REGULATION

"Keep your heart with all diligence, for out of it spring the issues of life."

Proverbs 4:23, NKJV

The Bible instructs us to guard our hearts because everything we do flows from it. It is true that the heart is tied to everything we do, including our financial decision-making. Some people talk about the battle between their heads and their hearts. Often, many of our financial decisions are intertwined in this emotional whirlwind, leaving us paralyzed and doubting the possibility of financial freedom and healing.

Maintaining emotional balance and understanding how finances work has a two-fold result. It allows us to rationally assess information and risk, and it also enables us to clearly and methodically process complex information. When it comes to regulating our emotions in an effort to be a wise steward over our finances, we must also attain the ability to effectively manage and respond to all types of emotional experiences.

Whenever high levels of stress keep us tied to emotional highs and lows, there is the possibility of shutting off areas of the brain required to make effective choices. Endorphins in your brain designed to block pain are also responsible for our feelings of pleasure, and they encourage us to go after whatever is needed to feel the associated pleasure.[1] The majority of our emotions and memories are processed by the brain's limbic system and include the region that handles a range of functions from breathing and sexual satisfaction to hunger and emotional response.

When everything is working normally, we can experience pleasure and a sense of satisfaction in a balanced way. But when we're stressed, those same chemicals can cause emotional highs and lows that are then often tied to our spending. Many people will buy to receive some type of gratification or exoneration because they are spending from a place of depression (low) or a desire for excess (high). If someone is going through a tough time, such as

Preface: The Heart of Your Finances

difficulty in a relationship, they may pacify themselves by going out and spending money because it makes them feel better.

There are emotional cues or clues to whether or not you are becoming anxious. In some instances, having a particular type of personality may make some people more predisposed to stress and worry than others. While some measure of day-to-day stress is considered normal, suffering from severe anxiety may be symptomatic of something serious. In these cases, it's important to talk with a mental health specialist about your symptoms.[2]

For example, those who suffer from anxiety attacks sometimes find themselves in a position where they cannot think or function normally. They're unable to change their financial deficiencies when they are that anxious. Their mind has been robbed of its peace to the point where their current state, unless properly addressed and treated, can become their ongoing reality.

On the other hand, the principle of being anxious for nothing can become a declarative statement of your determination to change your thinking, and as a result, your financial position—and that is what this book is about.

You can have hope and a healthy perspective about your finances! God's power and might is available to get you to a place of financial purpose, promise, and prominence.

Notes

1. Endorphins and Emotions. Tom Scheve. https://science.howstuffworks.com/life/inside-the-mind/emotions/endorphins1.htm
2. 7 Causes of Anxiety. Chris Iliades, MD. https://www.everydayhealth.com/anxiety-pictures/7-surprising-causes-of-anxiety.aspx

Chapter 1

Your First Investment

American culture generally takes an unconventional approach to informing how most people view their investments. Ninety-nine percent of those interested in financial investing have a mindset conditioned for Wall Street, in that they are accustomed to accepting the minimum amount for their returns. That conditioning gears us to believe that we need to save for 30 years toward our retirement, expecting to receive a return on our investment at a much later time.

The concern often not addressed is whether or not we will be healthy enough to enjoy a high quality of life, as well as the risk of there not being enough money available to live on upon retirement. A harsh reminder of this reality was the 2008 mortgage bank crisis when many people lost everything they had saved for their retirements.

Just as you should plan for an annual physical check-up to determine if there have been any new developments with your body, you should have a yearly check-up on your financial health. This includes not only checking your investments, but your credit-to-debt ratio, fluctuations in spending regarding how you use your credit cards, and any changes in the interest rates you are being charged for those cards.

This requires taking an intentional, holistic approach to your finances in terms of knowing where you are presently as well as where you are in relation to your future financial goals.

Setting homes and retirement accounts aside, the most valuable asset you own is the person staring back at you in the mirror, the investment called you.[1] Getting an education, for example, has the potential to increase your long-term value. However, the short-term reward of a summer job at a fast food establishment that becomes full-time and causes you to quit school could get in the way of being able to increase that value.

> **There is nothing you can change in your life unless you empower yourself to grow.**

There is nothing you can change in your life unless you empower yourself to grow. This means it is imperative to learn, be willing to embrace change, and alter how you think. It also means you need to be willing to take the time and effort to invest in yourself to achieve something meaningful for future growth.

From a financial perspective, the first requirement to achieve new growth potential comes in gaining an understanding of how you think about money. This includes the way your resources are made, how they can be saved, and how they can be measured. This investment in yourself requires direction and guidance best received from the Lord.

The Scriptures give us instruction about living in abundance, about ownership, about being lenders and not borrowers, and about owing no man. The Bible is clear that a life of financial struggle is not the life God desires for His people.

BLESSING AND ABUNDANCE

"Bring ye all the tithes into the storehouse, that there may be meat in mine house, and prove me now herewith, saith the Lord of hosts, if I will not open you the windows of heaven, and pour you out a blessing, that there shall not be room enough to receive it. And I will rebuke the devourer for your sakes, and he shall not destroy the fruits of your ground; neither shall your vine cast her fruit before the time in the field, saith the Lord of hosts. And all nations shall call you blessed: for ye shall be a delightsome land, saith the Lord of hosts."

Malachi 3:10-12, KJV

Financial Healing from the Inside Out

Blessing poured out from God that you do not have room enough to receive is the abundance that the Bible declares and that we have to train our minds to understand and expect. The Lord gives us instructions for how we are to live and possess the land. We should have an avenue that directs us toward His abundance and allows us to give generously toward God's Kingdom without feeling as though our giving will leave us in want.

There is a seven-fold blessing[2] associated with this passage of scripture from Malachi. These blessings illustrate God's intent and promised plan for your life as you obey Him with your finances:

1. See if I will not open you the windows of heaven… [v. 10]
2. …and pour you out a blessing that there shall not be room enough to receive. [v. 10]
3. I will rebuke the devourer for your sakes. [v. 11]
4. He shall not destroy the fruits of your ground. [v. 11]
5. Neither shall your vine cast her fruit before the time in the field. [v. 11]
6. All nations shall call you blessed. [v. 12]
7. You shall be "a delightsome land." [v. 12]

This clearly teaches that any curse of debt that may exist in your life will be broken by only one thing—giving to the Lord's work. It is the tithe that opens up Heaven, and it is your offering (the extra giving as the Lord directs you) that brings prosperity your way and to others as well. It is clear that God requires both the tithe and the offering. The tithe releases God's blessing, while the offering releases His abundance.

Your offering is that which is freely given by you to the work of the Lord. But offerings are more than just writing a check. Romans 12:1 exhorts us to offer our bodies as "a living sacrifice, holy, acceptable to God" (NKJV) as part of our worship. Romans 6:13 provides the reason why we are to offer ourselves: to be "instruments of righteousness to God." (NKJV)

Malachi 3:10 is the only place in the entire Bible where God challenges us to put *Him* to the test. Even more, He challenges us to prove Him *now*, meaning that His blessing is attached to a season. This season of blessing and outpouring begins with our faithful obedience to His Word.

"The Lord will open to you His good treasure, the heavens, to give the rain to your land in its season, and to bless all the work of your hand. You shall lend to many nations, but you shall not borrow. And the Lord will make you the head and not the tail; you shall be above only, and not be beneath, if you heed the commandments of the Lord your God, which I command you today, and are careful to observe them."

Deuteronomy 28:12-13, NKJV

Financial Healing from the Inside Out

You may believe everything feels good in your life right now because you possess what the world classifies as being good and are in a good place financially. However, it is still necessary to challenge yourself and continue aligning yourself to be able to journey "from glory to glory" (2 Corinthians 3:18) in God's Kingdom. This requires asking God how to get there.

One method for challenging yourself is to learn about financial principles. This does not require a great deal of money. There are unlimited resources in local libraries. You also have to refuse to be conditioned by the fabrications typically seen on reality television and in the movies. Instead, ask God to reveal the truth about finances that He has specifically for you by praying to Him and studying the Word of God. Refuse to just get by in life with mediocrity. Always seek to go a little deeper and strive to go a little higher than your counterparts. When this process feels like it's getting hard, continue to study and to press in. Don't give up when it gets tough.

Think of it as a child first learning how to walk. The early stages of a baby's development begin with learning to sit up, then starting to crawl. As she becomes stronger and more curious, the baby will pull herself up and get balanced by holding her parent's hand while taking a few steps. The next stage of development is cruising. This is where

Your First Investment

the baby starts to use the walls or furniture to get around, becoming more mobile and learning to stand without any help. The next stage is exploration, where she takes her unassisted first steps and is when a few stumbles and falls will occur. This is also the most exciting stage because the baby will continue to get up and keep trying until walking has been mastered.

There will be some moments in God's journey of blessing and abundance when you feel off balance, or when you take a step and fall. Yet that's not the time to become discouraged, but to keep trying until you have mastered it.

HIDDEN ANXIETIES MAY BIRTH FEAR

There is a difference between fear and anxiety. Normally, we can make a clear distinction between the two by understanding the simple linguistics. We say that we have a fear *of* something (such as a fear of flying), and we say that we have anxiety *about* something [such as anxiety about aging].[3] Other examples are the sudden rearrangement of your guts when an intruder holds a knife to your back (fear) that is far different from the butterflies in your stomach as you are about to make a difficult decision (anxiety). Anxiety describes a lingering apprehension or a chronic sense of worry or tension. Fear suggests something bigger and stronger than anxiety in terms of real-life experience.

Your understanding of what causes your anxiety comes when you realize you have fear about something that may occur in the future rather than something happening right now. Anxiousness may not have an on/off switch, but you can calm yourself in its midst.

The first step to vanquishing anxiety is to ask for help. The book of Proverbs encourages us to seek life-giving counsel. This is certainly appropriate if you believe anxiety is getting in the way of living your best life. The second step can be an affirmation prayer like the one from Proverbs 3:24 which states, "When you lie down, you will not be afraid; Yes, you will lie down and your sleep will be sweet." (NKJV) At the moment you start to feel anxious, recite a Bible scripture that helps you remember God's design for your life.

> **The first step to vanquishing anxiety is to ask for help.**

The Word of God offers spiritual remedies for those times when you are suffering from physical and emotional anxiety. Here are 11 quick anxiety relief tips:[4]

1. Praise breaths. Draw a breath using five counts, hold for five seconds, and then release (Psalm 150:6).

2. Prayer (1 John 5:14).
3. Time in the Word (Romans 12:2).
4. Self-care and relaxation (Matthew 11:28-30).
5. Limit distractions (Romans 8:6).
6. Exercise (Romans 12:1).
7. Healthy eating and getting enough protein (1 Corinthians 10:31).
8. Getting sleep (Proverbs 3:24).
9. Planning ahead (Psalm 37:5).
10. Being patient through the anxiety (Romans 5:2-4).
11. Holding on to victory through Christ (Luke 21:19).

WHO OWNS YOUR COMMON STOCK?

In the financial world, common stock represents the most common type of stock issued by companies. It entitles the company shareholders to participate in the profit and growth of the company in which they are investing.[5] In a corporation, for example, they control the Board of Directors and have voting rights.

When we think of this in terms of your personal life, common stockholders represent our ownership and to whom we have given up our rights and decision-making authority. When we allow friends to persuade us or others to tell us what we can or cannot do with our finances, they are then able to exercise control in the decision-making of our growth and future potential. When we are dependent upon others in order to move, then we have given up the common stock in our lives.

Some people may tend to keep us in a box according to their own growth. Therefore, if an individual says to you, "It doesn't take all that," then it is most likely because it really does not take all that for them. However, it may very well take all that in order for you to grow and go to the place where you are destined to be financially.

Who have you allowed to come in and make decisions for you? To whom have you given up your rights in order to function? Who have you allowed to rob you of your aspirations and your dreams?

WHO OWNS YOUR PREFERRED STOCK?

Preferred stockholders in the financial world typically have first access when it comes to dividends or in a bankruptcy situation where, after creditors are paid, preferred stockholders are compensated before common shareholders. Preferred stock can also have set terms where a holder can have them redeemed at a favorable price for cash or sometimes even common shares.[6]

Your personal preferred stockholders should be those individuals who hold the greatest value

Your First Investment

to your life. They share in your financial dreams and aspirations, and they continually pray for you, encourage you, and hold you accountable. Your preferred stockholders will remind you who you are in God and whose you are. They will exhort you that God is the One who is going to lead and direct you. They may be your preachers, your teachers, your mentors—or your financial consultants.

Be encouraged to take a careful and prayerful assessment of whom you are giving ownership of your preferred stock. In addition, evaluate and list those who are blocking you and not building you up. You can consider this your "velvet rope" list, people who are cordoned off and have limited access to you while you walk along the red carpet of your journey to financial freedom. These might be relatives, business associates, or friends who shout from behind the rope, "You can't do it!" "You won't make it." "You'll never be successful!" Keep them at a distance and don't allow them to deter you.

As an investor, the decision between investing in common stock vs. preferred stock often comes down to an assessment of risk and reward. Common stock is chancier: you may lose it all, but it often provides a better chance to participate in the growth of a successful company. Preferred stock is less risky but comes with set dividend and repayment terms.

Ultimately, the choice comes down to weighing your opinion on the future of the company you are considering for investment.[7] That is also the case with your personal common or preferred stockholders. Choose them wisely, for they will impact your future financial success.

WHAT FREEDOM LOOKS AND FEELS LIKE

"Jesus answered them, 'Most assuredly, I say to you, whoever commits sin is a slave of sin. And a slave does not abide in the house forever, but a son abides forever. Therefore if the Son makes you free, you shall be free indeed.'"

John 8:34-36, NKJV

Children of God abide in the house of God. As such, they don't have to abide on the outside as a part of the world system because they are in the King's system. As a believer, financial freedom gives you the ability to do what you know you ought to do—and to do whatever God wants you to do because you trust and believe that He has already taken care of it. It isn't necessary to be looking over your shoulder in fear, concerned about any creditors or debtors. This freedom gives you liberty because you know that God's resources are available and that they are in perfect alignment with whatever He says is needed for His Kingdom.

Your First Investment

Financial freedom emancipates you from the emotional burden of your possessions. John 10:10 says Satan's plan is to steal, kill, and destroy. He doesn't want your stuff. He is fully aware you can acquire more of that. His intent is to attack your peace. A friend who is a pastor once said, "If the enemy is allowed to gain a toehold in your life, then this can lead to his ability to gain to a foothold, which then has the ability to allow him to gain a stronghold." The devil knows how attached we can become to our money and our things; therefore, if he can succeed in undermining your peace, he can stagnate your growth. When you have no peace, you will be up at night pacing the floor, anxious and weary.

We are not to be ignorant of the enemy's devices. This is why it is imperative that you invest in yourself so that you will not be attached to your possessions, and listen to the Word of God as it instructs you how to be financially free.

Notes

1. Your Most Valuable Asset is Yourself. Carl Richards. https://www.nytimes.com/2015/12/15/your-money/your-most-valuable-asset-is-yourself.html
2. Seven Blessings of the Tithe. Benny Hinn. https://cfctyger.wordpress.com/2013/05/01/seven-blessings-of-the-tithe-by-benny-hinn/
3. Fear vs. Anxiety. Harriet Lerner, Ph.D. https://www.psychologytoday.com/us/blog/the-dance-connection/200910/fear-vs-anxiety
4. Unmasking the Mess. https://unmaskingthemess.com/anxiety-remedies/
5. Common Stock. http://www/investorguide.com/article/15593/common-stock-vs-preferred-stock-d1412/
6. Ibid
7. Ibid

Chapter 2

Rebellion and Control

The Bible tells you to forsake rebellion, warning us that it'll darken your spiritual eyesight and deafen your spiritual ears. Rebellion undermines your discernment and reduces your ability to hear God's voice—and that leaves you vulnerable to make poor choices in all areas of your life, including with your finances.

"He brings out those who are bound into prosperity; But the rebellious dwell in a dry land."

Psalm 68:6, NKJV

"You dwell in the midst of a rebellious house, which has eyes to see but does not see, and ears to hear but does not hear."

Ezekiel 12:2, NKJV

Financial Healing from the Inside Out

When in rebellion, we choose to do what is wrong while simultaneously knowing what is right. We may have even been taught about the proper use of money, but in a rebellious state, wise decisions about spending or saving will not be made. Rebellion often manifests when what is comfortable is preferred over the harder decision that'll actually change our financial position for the better. We look only at what can be obtained in the moment rather than choosing to use our money as a catalyst to succeed later.

Let's say you've made a conscious decision not to pay your rent on time so that you can splurge on some new clothes or to buy a new gaming system or big-screen television. You know you are in rebellion to your responsibility to take care of the rent, but figure you'll get the money somehow, pay it late, and all will be well. Surely, there won't be any serious repercussions, right?

Then you receive an eviction notice—the consequence of your rebellious actions. Instantly, you go to the landlord and beg for more time, but your pleas are ignored. Now you have more clothes in your closet or a new entertainment system in the living room, but you have to move out because you failed in your responsibility. What you thought was going to bring happiness has now made you sad and stressed because you have to find a new place to live before the end of

Rebellion and Control

the month. In addition, the eviction means you won't be getting your security deposit back, but you will now have to come up with that amount, plus the first month's rent, in order to move in to another apartment.

Another form of rebellion with money is financial infidelity—where someone, unknown to their spouse, partner, or significant other, secretly spends cash, uses a credit card, or holds hidden accounts where they are borrowing money. Incredibly, for every five American couples with combined finances, two of them have, at some point, committed financial infidelity.[1] Some people have found out that their partners had hundreds of thousands of dollars of debt they didn't know about. As you'd imagine, these relationships experience massive stress, unhappiness, and betrayal of trust, effecting all areas of their lives. Some end up in divorce.

Scripture declares that our stubborn opposition and defiant resistance to the One who is in authority will cause us to be unsuccessful, and our refusal to accept and obey the prescribed standards of behavior found in the Bible carries the penalty of rejection by God, leaving us "in a dry land" where we will not prosper. Any tendency to make a selfish or unwise purchase, especially during times of financial struggle, must be offset with the wisdom and discipline to prioritize paying our bills and taking care of the things we need.

We simply cannot throw caution to the wind and later justify it by saying, "I'll never be able to catch up anyway, so I might as well just keep on doing it." That is not the mindset of a responsible individual, and that person may need deliverance from God in order that he be kept from rebellion.

RELINQUISHING YOUR DESIRE TO PLEASE YOURSELF OR OTHERS

"For am I now seeking the approval of man, or of God? Or am I trying to please man? If I were still trying to please man, I would not be a servant of Christ."

Galatians 1:10, ESV

To relinquish means to give up control, possession, or power over something. It also means to renounce something by leaving it behind and letting it go. When we rebel and hold on to our finances in a way that is not pleasing to God, we are undermining our own strength by letting money have power over us. Even more, when we choose to use money to please ourselves or others, we will continuously find ourselves running after something we can never truly possess.

The desire to please someone else, or even to please ourselves, with money may come from wanting to maintain a particular appearance or lifestyle that is outside of our financial scope. Whether it's to look a certain way or maintain a certain status in order to get the attention of others or appear successful, we may have to use funds that should otherwise not be spent. An example would be to purchase high-end, expensive designer shoes and clothes for yourself and your children in an attempt to meet a particular socio-economic standard instead of shopping at Walmart.

> **To relinquish means to give up control, possession, or power over something.**

When you need to be obedient and disciplined to operate within a specific spending plan, it is acceptable and wise to not try to appear to be wealthy. It is also permissible and smart to be strategic in the use of your money so that your finances can grow, rather than to remain under the stigma of others viewing you as though you possess something substantial. You must consider how your spending decisions will affect you over the long-term.

Over the past few decades, credit cards have become the default way the majority of Americans pay for their purchases. However, that method of payment comes with certain difficulties and responsibilities that you have to be able to manage. Be aware that credit card use may place you in perpetual bondage to your debt—which is exactly what the credit card companies want you to do.

Here are some of the untruths we tell ourselves about credit cards:[2]

Untruth #1: I'll get a cash advance just this one time

If you're in a tough spot, getting a cash advance seems like a great solution. However, the credit card company charges a fee for that advance, and they will probably raise your interest rate as well. Always shop around and ask questions before entering into an agreement with a lender. Be aware of the *total* payment amount over the life of a loan or credit transaction, because borrowing more than is affordable is never a good decision. In addition, avoid promises to refinance your credit at better rates in the future. There is never a guarantee that interest rates can be reduced later.

Untruth #2: I hate to look at my statement

Most people don't bother looking at their statements because they have a hard time discerning the information, but reading and understanding your statement is critical, especially if you have been double-charged somewhere or if your account has been hacked. In addition, making late payments or going over your credit limit will, usually unbeknownst to you, give the credit card company the right to increase your interest rate. In fact, some credit card companies participate in predatory lending practices by targeting consumers they have previously determined as being more unlikely to be able to make their payments on time.

Untruth #3: I can afford the minimum payments

We pay minimum payments believing they will keep us current, overlooking the fact that paying the minimum may take you decades to fully pay off the debt, and will result in you paying many times more than the original amount of the purchase if you had used cash.

Untruth #4: I'll use a credit card to get rewards

Airline miles and rebates are enticements to get you to use the card more often. It's easy to convince yourself that the reward of a plane ticket for your vacation will help you to forget about your debt problems. It might cause you to forget for a while, but it'll still be there—and be larger—when you get back.

Untruth #5: I'll never make a late payment

Here, you reason that if there's not enough money in your account to make the payment, when it is due you can simply make that payment using another card that has a later date. That will only exacerbate your problem, not resolve it.

Untruth #6: I'll never exceed my credit limit

You may mean this, too—until a good reason comes along. Often it is to cover a legitimate emergency expense, but sometimes you could justify doing it because of a blowout sale on shoes where you just have to get *that* pair. In either case, it's easy to convince yourself the purchase was worth the cost of the extra fees and higher interest rate.

Untruth #7: I'll only use it for emergencies

See Untruth #6.

Tens of thousands of people are in bondage to credit card payments and high interest rates. The terms of a credit card payment may last for years, during which you are actually chasing and trying to hold onto that possession. Unfortunately, when you chase the dollar, you also relentlessly look for ways to make more income or find more avenues to create more money just to be able to sustain an idea of wealth instead of actually being disciplined and accepting a process that you have to go through in order to attain actual wealth.

If you believe that you have been enticed and fallen victim to the enthrallment of credit cards, it may be necessary for you to seek financial coaching about how to do better research, become credit card savvy, and understand how to manage your finances.

GIVING GOD CONTROL

Relinquishing your desires will require embracing what God has for you and allowing Him to take control over your life, trusting and believing that He never fails and has the ability to take care of you. It won't happen overnight, but keep going and don't give up, using the words of the following verse as inspiration:

> *"I can do all things through him who strengthens me."*
> **Philippians 4:13, ESV**

Simply put, control is to have power over something. As humans, we *love* to have control over the things that we do. We love to have a plan. We've grown up hearing advice such as, "You can do anything you set your mind to do. Just follow your heart!" Nevertheless, when things don't go the way we planned, we can feel disappointed, unfulfilled, anxious, and even angry. For Christians, the process of relinquishing control and giving it to God takes several measured steps:

1. **Let go.** Luke 9:23 instructs us to deny ourselves, take up Christ's cross daily, and follow Him. This means we are to "die to Jesus" by surrendering our wants and desires—our very lives—to Him. Galatians 5:24 affirms this by saying "those who are Christ's have crucified the flesh with its passions and desires." (NKJV) This may sound very difficult, and it isn't easy, but when we commit our lives to God and allow Him to take control, He not only reveals what we should let go of, but He promises to be with us all the way through the process.

2. **Obey fully.** There will be times when the Lord tells us to do something that may not seem logical. He may command us to take a plunge at something completely new. This can be scary, but whenever God tells you to do something, particularly

with your finances, just do it. Be diligent. Follow through. Don't try to find a middle ground between what you want and what He wants. Remember, half obedience is still *disobedience*. We hinder God's blessing for our lives when we only give him half of our obedience. He wants it all—and deserves nothing less.

3. **Expect warfare.** The Christian life is not perfect, and contrary to popular belief, followers of God are warned to *expect* trials. Why? As we get closer to God, we become a bigger threat to Satan, so the enemy is going to do anything possible to make us fall. We are called to be vigilant, to pray continuously, and read the Word of God. We must seek God daily and not trust only in ourselves or anyone else. If we do not do this, life's circumstances will take us off guard and knock us off our feet. Psalm 37:23-24 tell us that God makes firm the steps of the one who delights in Him. Even though we may stumble, He never fails and upholds us with His hand.

4. **Don't compare yourself to others.** Sometimes we see others being successful financially and we ask the Lord, "What about me?" Yet we are not to concern ourselves with what others have. Author Os

Hillman teaches that God has called us to a unique life that may look totally different from anyone else's life, and that once we begin to compare ourselves to others, we begin to live for others and ourselves.[3] Another reason to shun comparison is the fact that we cannot know everything that an individual has had to walk through in order to receive what they have been given. You don't know their story, nor do you know the challenges that were before them or what they had to press through in order to attain their blessings. Instead, embrace and protect the life that God has for you. He knows exactly what you need. Don't envy others. That is their life; this is yours. Trust that God knows your every desire and *wants* to bless you.

> **We are not to concern ourselves with what others have.**

5. **Don't doubt God's ability.** It's easy to look at our circumstances and become anxious if things don't go as planned. Likewise, being uncertain about our future can cause us to worry. Therefore, if we find it hard to trust that God is in control of our lives, we don't have peace. But in Psalm 46:10 we are encouraged

Rebellion and Control

to "be still and know" that He is God. Jeremiah 29:11 adds, "'For I know the plans I have for you,' declares the Lord, 'plans to prosper you and not to harm you, plans to give you hope and a future.'" God knows what you need, and He knows when you need it.

6. **Rid yourself of presumptions.** In Numbers 14, the people of God were told to conquer the land, but they doubted. They were afraid, so they didn't do as God commanded. They didn't embrace God's plan and they didn't trust Him to take care of them. They assumed control, presuming they could do it. As a result, even after God had warned He would not be with them, they trusted in their own strength and tried to conquer the land without Him. They lost the battle.

    When we make presumptions, we think, "If God was with me, then this *shouldn't* have happened," or, "If this was truly God's will, then this and that *should* have happened by now." Whenever we start to assume or overthink the details in our lives, we have to stop and be reminded that God's thoughts and ways are not like ours (Isaiah 55:8-9).

7. **Really enjoy life!** Seek to be thankful, embrace that which God has called and

purposed in you, and trust Him. Psalm 37:4 reminds you to delight yourself in the Lord and that He will give you the desires of your heart. Proverbs 16:20 lets you know that whoever trusts in the Lord will be happy. Nehemiah 8:10 declares that the joy of the Lord is your strength.

Take these principles and these promises, make them your own, and give God control of your life and your finances. You'll never be the same when you do!

LEARNING TO TAKE THE HIGH ROAD

"Do not be conformed to this world, but be transformed by the renewal of your mind, that by testing you may discern what is the will of God, what is good and acceptable and perfect."

Romans 12:2, ESV

Taking the high road means that you are choosing to make the correct decision and to follow a course of action that will be the least harmful or upsetting. The high road is generally the road less traveled and least trendy. The trendy road is usually the one seen as being fashionable and up-to-date, the place of influence and style. Yet trendy is defined

Rebellion and Control

as something ephemeral, superficial, or a passing fad. It doesn't last.

People often engage in certain activities because it appears to be the trendy thing to do. However, some are done without consideration of the risk or danger. The Madoff investment scandal was a major case of stock and securities fraud discovered in late 2008 that several investors thought was the good and trendy thing to do—until they lost all of their money.

Taking the high road with your finances may include carving off as much fat from your spending plan as you can. This requires making a decision to be disciplined with your finances, concentrating on how and why you are spending in order to gain a deeper understanding about how a spending plan can work for you. Staying on a spending plan is a true challenge—but it's one that can be compromised by the trendy road paved with brand name advertising.

Brand name products have been ingrained and cultivated in American culture for the better part of the last century. Brand names like Coca-Cola and Kleenex surround us every day, and in the same way babies have learned to speak certain words by repeating them, adults do the same with brand name products. This kind of word association gives businesses a lot of control over how people interpret their brands. If they're successful, we learn to mentally link a brand name and associate it with good things. Merchants rely on the fact that a particular brand name will be associated with positive emotions. They count on having a lifelong customer as a result.

Therefore, buying particular products is tied to our emotions. Not only have certain product names been entrenched in our memories, the appeal of certain items to maintain a particular image or lifestyle has been established as well. If you want Gucci or Giorgio Armani, then nothing else will do. If it's Nike or nothing else, you'll likely never frequent the discount sneaker store. Yet the transformation in your thinking that leads to deliverance from financial rebellion will not happen if your perceived brand loyalty dictates your buying decisions and perceived emotional well-being.

Brand loyalty may be just one of the barriers that need to be eliminated in your life in order for you to take the high road financially. It requires a great deal of discipline and a lack of fear of the changes that need to take place. The high road may require you to reexamine the social status you desire, but it will take you to the place where you can achieve your financial freedom.

True wealth is not only money and resources. It is a mindset. Once the high road takes you to its final destination, you'll realize that it isn't necessary to try to look wealthy physically on the outside because you will actually be wealthy spiritually on the inside.

Notes

1. Financial Infidelity. Alexia Elejalde-Ruiz, Tribune Newspapers. https://www.chicagotribune.com/lifestyles/sc-cons-0210-save-financial-infidelit20110211-story.html
2. 7 Huge Credit Card Lies We Tell Ourselves. http://www.cfinancialfreedom.com/7-huge-credit-card-lies-we-tell-ourselves/
3. Os Hillman Speaking and Teaching Messages. http://www.marketplaceleaders.org/speakingmessage/

Chapter 3

Gaining a Wealthy Mindset

People define wealth different ways. It could be the accumulation of money, good physical health, or the achievement of a certain lifestyle. Regardless of what you believe it means to be wealthy, it all boils down to the idea of living beyond an average or mediocre state of existence.

With that in mind, it is important to understand what it takes to develop a wealthy mindset—because you can then conform your thinking to welcome the idea of wealth in your life. Jaime Tardy, a business coach who helps entrepreneurs achieve their goals and author of *The Eventual Millionaire*, says the wealthy succeed because they don't let money control them, but are in control of their money.

The wealthy are solution-based people who weigh the ramifications of their decisions. They focus on the forces that work in their favor and understand the factors that can come against them. Wealthy people understand the five elements that continually challenge their financial well-being and ability to make more money—taxes, regulations, inflation, the depreciation of the dollar, and risks—and they strategically develop a financial plan that will circumvent them.

Some people, for example, do not realize how often they are taxed. Not only can you pay federal taxes each year when you file your tax return, but you are taxed for your earned income every time you receive a paycheck. There are sometimes taxes paid to your home state, and you may also pay property taxes on your home. As a result of this multiple taxation, many tend to feel defeated because they pay so much money. Yet the wealthy understand there are ways within the law to either avoid certain taxes or pay less overall, and they employ these strategies to their benefit.

By employing the assistance of a certified public accountant (CPA) or financial health coach, you can utilize these strategies to not pay as much in taxes as you are now. But a CPA or coach aren't the only people who can help you attain a wealthy mindset. Getting the advice of someone who has gone before you and is now prospering is far better than listening to someone operating on your same level who will say, "You don't need to do that," or, "I wouldn't focus on that if I were you." That type of thinking is not solution-based or forward-looking.

Therefore, cultivate and maintain a circle of influence who will cause you to reach a little higher. This goes back to the stakeholders we mentioned earlier in the book. Choose to be around people who will help you progress and succeed financially, not hold you back.

When it comes to financial investing, clients are asked to describe their risk tolerance, defined as how much they can stand to lose on a given investment strategy and portfolio. This helps clients and their financial advisor decide whether a particular investment is good or bad, based on the amount of risk they're willing to take. Properly assessing different options and their risk requires you to educate yourself about investments, so you can choose the right ones to best achieve your financial goals, and then track the performance of those risks with a solution-based mindset.

The wealthy never place all their eggs in one basket. They diversify their portfolios to include investments carrying various risk/reward potential. They either personally possess a strong knowledge about investments such as certificates of deposit (CDs), individual retirement accounts (IRAs), or a tax-qualified, defined-contribution pension account [401(k)], or they hire advisors or coaches who do. Diversification of your investments starts with getting advice from a financial professional who can help you understand and use the different tools available to you to best utilize your *passive* income so that you can be in a position to make money while you sleep. This is what the wealthy do, and it is vital to your future financial freedom.

What is passive income?[1] Active income is when you do the work and get paid for that work. If you work for McDonald's, you are paid for the hours you are there. If you work in an office, you may not clock in or clock out, but you are paid based on the work you do. In either case, if you do no work, you will not be paid. Passive income, however, is money you receive that is not directly tied to active work. Interest and dividends earned are examples of passive income.

> The wealthy never place all their eggs in one basket.

Typical passive income sources are front-loaded with active work, for which you are paid a small amount, while the bulk of the income made comes later. Passive income still requires work, but everything you earn is not directly tied to the hours worked. Anyone who owns rental properties knows that it's considered passive income, but there is quite a bit of work involved, yet the owner

Gaining a Wealthy Mindset

is able to collect rent checks on an individual unit for many months before having to reengage with work on that unit.

Take a look at the Robert Kiyosaki Cashflow Quadrant.[2] It sums up the essence of financial success.[3] The left side of the quadrant shows how you can make a good income, while the right side focuses on how you can become wealthy. Most people use only income to make money, pay their taxes, and then spend the rest. But those operating with passive income make money, spend it, and *then* pay their taxes. This simple difference is huge and can be the biggest weapon for success in your financial arsenal.

ACTIVE INCOME	PASSIVE INCOME
Employee **E** [You have job security] No leverage	**Business Owner** **B** [You own a system] Leverage
Self Employed **S** [You own a job] Trading time for money	**Investor** **I** [Money works for you] Income not depending on your presence
When work stops, income stops	When work stops, income continues to create wealth

FINANCIAL HEALING FROM THE INSIDE OUT

In addition to investment strategy and use of passive income, a spending plan will help you properly spend, save, and give of your money, as well as learn important things such as the interest attached to your debt payments. This will help you begin to calculate and decrease how much interest you are paying out each month. Interest is a way your wealth is transferred away from you that you can correct and reassign to passive income that will earn wealth for you.

Not surprisingly, the teachings of Jesus were solution-based. It was how He talked and walked throughout His brief time in public ministry.

Whenever Christ saw a problem, He did not ask why it was a problem; He prayed to the Father, asked for a solution, and then did only what He saw the Father do. If He needed to go deeper with people, Jesus declared what the Father was thinking and helped them apply that to their everyday lives. The Lord looked at a problem and came up with the solution—be it healing, deliverance, wisdom, or even money.

"Let this mind be in you which was also in Christ Jesus."
Philippians 2:5, NKJV

Here are six tips to developing a wealthy mindset:[4]

1. **Believe that you deserve wealth.** If you don't believe this, you will sabotage your efforts. Wanting to attract wealth but

Gaining a Wealthy Mindset

not believing you deserve it is like trying to drive a car while pressing both the accelerator and the brake at the same time. It will get you nowhere.

2. **Develop an "opportunity consciousness."** Look around and begin to ask yourself, "How can I add more value or solve a particular problem—and make money while doing it?" The bigger the problems you solve, the more wealth will pour into your life. The more you serve others, the more wealth you will achieve.

3. **Organize your life to matter more to others**. The more you make your time and life valuable to those around you, the more wealth you will gain. Develop valuable skills, network with high achievers, and focus on serving people.

4. **Begin to think in terms of passive income**. If you are continually selling your time in exchange for money, then your income is limited because your time is limited.

5. **Visualize wealth**. See yourself making money. Visualize total financial abundance flowing toward you. You can tap into this vision.

6. **Cancel out negative thoughts**. Guard your thinking. If you allow garbage into

your mind, you'll get garbage results. If you have great ideas, you'll get great results. Monitor your internal dialogue and what other people are saying to you, especially regarding wealth.

MULTIPLE STREAMS OF INCOME

As you become educated about finances and adopt a solution-based mindset, you also discover that it takes at least seven streams of income to become wealthy and then strategically utilize your family and their lives to build legacies of wealth. The key to accumulating wealth is uncomplicated: 1) sell your time for money, 2) spend less than you earn, and 3) invest your savings so that it will grow without your active intervention.

Some of the most common income streams for millionaires include the following:

- Interest from a variety of loans either to individuals (peer-to-peer lending or private notes) or companies (bonds, notes).
- Dividends from investments and partnerships.
- Capital gains from the sale of investments.
- Royalties from products you sell or license.
- Rental income from real estate.
- Business income which may or may not be

Gaining a Wealthy Mindset

passive, but the idea is to build something that generates income without active work, such as the sale of informational products through a website.

Other streams of income include:

- Compound interest earned from a single deposit into an interest-bearing account that has been sitting undisturbed for a period of time.
- Investing, commonly done through a portfolio of high dividend-paying stocks or peer-to-peer lending where you loan money and get paid back interest through an automated system.
- Some life insurance policies that are compound interest earning.
- Hobbies. You may be unaware of an untapped gift God has birthed within you that can allow you to earn income while doing something you love.
- Your savings.
- Your giving. One of the hardest concepts for some people to grasp is the path of "giving" your way into wealth. As mentioned earlier, God will bless your giving and return it to you in abundance. Some give tithes or offerings from what

is left over after everything else has been taken care of—but giving first before paying for anything else will display your obedience to Him and release God's Spirit in you and in your finances.

"Give, and it will be given to you: good measure, pressed down, shaken together, and running over will be put into your bosom. For with the same measure that you use, it will be measured back to you."

Luke 6:38, NKJV

When we give, God gives back to us. He also helps us discern right from wrong and will let us know the paths that are best for us as we begin to use a wealthy mindset to inform what we do with our money. When we believe with our whole hearts that God made us to be blessed and blessed us to be a blessing, then we are positioned to ask God to show us His paths of financial blessing and how we can follow them.

"Now may He who supplies seed to the sower, and bread for food, supply and multiply the seed you have sown and increase the fruits of your righteousness"

2 Corinthians 9:10, NKJV

When you believe this passage and cheerfully give, He will then give you even more seed because

He can trust you. You have developed a wealth mindset fit for His Kingdom. Consequently, from your abundance, you can then help the community and build what He is doing in the earthly realm. Then He will say, "Well done, good and faithful servant; you have been faithful over a few things, I will make you ruler over many things. Enter into the joy of your lord." (Matthew 25:23, NKJV) If you want God to trust you with the wealth of His Kingdom, it's imperative that you give.

> **When we give, God gives back to us.**

FINANCIAL MATURITY = FINANCIAL STABILITY

Financial maturity comes as the result of four elements that lead to confidence.[5] The first is to educate yourself in the areas of personal finance. While you don't have to become an investment expert, you should have a working knowledge of your personal financial issues.

Secondly, you need to prepare yourself. As you save and accumulate assets, you also need to get a firm understanding of the total expenses required to support your lifestyle. How much is enough to save and accumulate for financial independence is directly dependent on how much you spend.

Third, exercise the discipline of sticking to a spending plan. This discipline results in freedom and peace of mind. Just as your social freedom depends on rules of law that serve a greater purpose, so, too, does your financial freedom. The discipline to live within your means supports the greater purpose of creating the freedom to spend your future days pursuing the activities you choose.

The final element is to have a healthy relationship with money. Virtually every major decision you make involves some consideration of the monetary consequences. What you do, where you live, and with whom you associate are all impacted by your mindset about money. Often, those attitudes and beliefs come from your childhood or cultural experiences that taint your perspective. Examining the source of our mindset allows you to discard thinking that no longer serves your purpose, allowing you to create a new set of attitudes and beliefs that are aligned with your transformed, Kingdom-focused values and purposes.

A WEALTHY MINDSET PRAYER

Go before the Lord now, telling Him how you are ready to walk through the process of becoming solution-based and to navigate from where you are now to the place He has purposed you to be.

Gaining a Wealthy Mindset

Dear God,

I bless You because I know that You want this for me. I choose to let go and relinquish everything associated with my past. I also relinquish everything associated with not being wealthy like You have called me to be so that I can do exactly what You have called me to do.

Here I am, God. Send me. Give through me. Live through me. Enliven me and allow me to do this for Your Kingdom.

In Jesus' name. Amen.

Notes

1. 7 Income Streams of Millionaires. Jim Wang. https://wallethacks.com/7-income-sources-streams-of-millionaires/
2. Robert Kiyosaki's Cash Flow Quadrant. https://www.knowledgebringsmoney.com/cash-flow-quadrant.html
3. Tax-Free Wealth: How to Build Massive Wealth by Permanently Lowering Your Taxes. http://successprogress.com/videos/taxfree/taxfree.pdf
4. How to Develop a "Wealth" Mindset. https://www.selfgrowth.com/articles/Sayre5.html.
5. What is Financial Maturity? Keith Weber. http://www.rethinkingretirement.com/article.php?id=85

Chapter 4

Reviving Your Financial Future

If you, or someone you know, has ever been in a place of pervasive drought and deadness regarding personal and financial life, know this: health and healing are available through the revival of our financial future. Through obedience to God's Word—and the instructions given in the following declaration and prophecy—there will be a blessed outpouring.

"Here is My weather forecast, Beloved. I AM coming to you like the Rain.

This outpouring will be record setting. Get ready to sing in the Rain. Get ready to dance.

Get ready to jump with joy. Get ready to smile and laugh again, Dear One.

Financial Healing from the Inside Out

I AM reviving, resuscitating, and restoring you, My Child. The enemy tried to lull you to sleep, steal your confidence, and wear you out. He comes but for to kill, steal and destroy.

But I have come to you, Dear One, bringing abundant, overflowing LIFE.

I AM resuscitating you with the Breath of Life. No longer shall you feel like the "walking dead." Oh no, My Love, you are ALIVE as I AM ALIVE.

Because I live, you will LIVE also. I AM bringing you back from the brink of death. I have crushed the head and the hand of the devil. He was leading you to destruction, My Child.

But no longer shall his hand be upon you. You are Mine. I take you in MY Hand.

Even now, I am breathing NEW LIFE into you by My Spirit.

Receive this heavenly outpouring, Beloved, straight from my Throne of Grace.

Fear not. My coming is as sure as the dawn. I AM coming to you like the Rain, like the spring showers that water the land."[1]

THREE STEPS TO FINANCIAL REVIVAL

Reviving means that there will be a refreshing, an enlivening, and a regaining of consciousness, breathing new life into one suffering an apparent death. In your finances, revival begins as you stop giving life to dead things in your relationships, your physical life, your spiritual life, and in how you handle your money. It all starts with three vital steps:

Step #1 – Seek wise counsel.

"Plans fail for lack of counsel, but with many advisers they succeed."

Proverbs 15:22, NIV

There are times when we will make a decision that we later regret. It is important to know where to seek wise and sound advice and how to discern it.[2] First, pray for God's guidance in finding the right person. Often, we'll have a particular type of person in mind who we believe will give us the advice we need, but the Lord may very well lead us to someone we did not anticipate who is a person of great godly wisdom (Proverbs 1:5). Next,

> **In your finances, revival begins as you stop giving life to dead things.**

develop an awareness of those around you. The wise counselor or mentor that God leads you to may be one who has withstood the tests of life, and time has taught them how to confidently place their whole trust in the sovereignty of God. It may not be someone who appears to have been endowed with superior spirituality (Proverbs 12:26).

Next, test your relationship over time. Your choice must be someone who has endured the trials of life yet remained true to the Lord. They are not perfect, but they are being perfected daily through Christ (1 Kings 20:11). Then confirm with the person you chose that they are to play this significant role in your life. The individual who mentors you must be ready for the responsibility and be able to hear from the Holy Spirit and share God's Word liberally and specifically with you (1 Corinthians 11:1).

A good mentor has the following characteristics:

- Knowledge (Proverbs 24:4). This person knows the Word of God and is well acquainted with sound teaching. They stick to the solid truths of the Bible and resist trends of "new" teachings.
- Wisdom (Proverbs 10:14). This person applies the knowledge of God's Word in their everyday interactions with family, friends, and strangers. Their lives are

Reviving Your Financial Future

marked with the seasoning of careful reasoning and understanding.
- Experience (1 Timothy 3:6). This person must have life experiences that have proven perseverance in the faith. A new convert needs more time to mature in the Christian faith.
- Discernment (Philippians 1:10). This person discerns what is good and right through the Scriptures and prayer. The Holy Spirit gives insight and direction to those who have fully submitted their lives to Christ.
- Truthfulness (Ephesians 4:15). This person will speak the hard truth to you in love. They want you to live righteously and avoid the pitfalls of ignorance.
- Compassion (Colossians 3:12). This person is marked by their love and compassion for God's people. Their speech and actions reflects the love of Christ.
- Integrity (2 Corinthians 1:12). This person strives to live a life of integrity, even when the world belittles their stance for what is right. They refuse to compromise or bow down to complicity or make excuses to justify themselves.
- Reputation (Proverbs 22:1). This person secures their reputation by making everyday

choices that reflect the grace and mercy given to them by Christ. They make great efforts to reveal the influence of Jesus on their lives.

Step #2 – Owe no man.

"Owe no one anything, except to love each other, for the one who loves another has fulfilled the law."

Romans 13:8, ESV

Pull your credit report and find out the details of every debt you owe so that you can then plan how to decrease or get out of debt entirely, in obedience to the biblical principle. You'll discover your credit history and payment habits, as created and maintained by credit reporting agencies. The three major credit bureaus in the United States are Equifax, Experian, and TransUnion.

Be aware that organizations or individuals such as banking institutions, landlords, government agencies, and even other credit agencies frequently refer to credit reports to determine whether or not a person qualifies for a loan, a new bank account, or to obtain a credit card. A good credit score is your avenue for getting competitive interests rates for such things as mortgages, cars, credit cards, and even insurance premiums. A strong score is worth money in the long run because it saves you from having to pay excessive costs to have and use credit or make a loan payment.

Once you have your credit report, thoroughly review it to learn all the creditors listed on the report. You should know and understand that you determine your credit score through your behavior managing debt, and that you have more than one credit score. Since the credit information obtained by each of the three credit agencies is different, the scores for each of those agencies is different. In addition, if you are applying for a loan, lenders may use a different score for the different types of loans available.

Step #3 – Create a spending plan.

The findings of your credit report will build the foundation for the development of a spending plan to eliminate debt and revive your financial future. Your spending plan will also facilitate accurate communication with your financial coach or mentor, as well as give you accountability and provide reasons why you cannot spend money for something that is not needed. With a spending plan, you will then be positioned to act.

"Arise! For this matter is your responsibility, but we will be with you; be courageous and act."

Ezra 10:4, NASB

"I heard the voice of the Lord, saying, Whom shall I send, and who will go for us? Then said I, Here am I; send me."

Isaiah 6:8, KJV

Financial Healing from the Inside Out

NO-thing happens unless you **DO** something. There has to be movement. Here are six indicators that it is time for you to make a change.[3]

1. **You forgot that you have choices.** Learn to recognize when enough is enough. Sometimes you have to stop hitting your head against the proverbial wall and move on. You don't have to continue living in the midst of drama just because it's familiar. Allow yourself to let go of people, situations, ideas, and feelings that aren't conducive to the nourishment of your growth or your soul. Commit to making choices that nurture your personal growth, give yourself permission to start a new chapter in your life, and make decisions that liberate you from following the wrong path and the wrong purpose.
2. **You forgot that you deserve the best.** Not everyone sees you through the same eyes, but everyone deserves to have someone in their corner who appreciates them just as they are. If you're besieged by people who are discouraging and critical, then the spark of inspiration and hope that allows you to be in touch with your deepest potential is crushed. You deserve to be appreciated and valued as God has ordained.

Surrounding yourself with those who have a constructive attitude will help you follow your path towards greater success and financial freedom.

3. **You let minor irritations become major problems**. Free yourself from those small annoyances that get you down. Life will consistently deliver challenges, and how you respond to them is entirely in your hands. Begin each day by practicing how to release something that you normally would find irritating. As you do, you will discover that you are freeing yourself to broaden your control over other areas of your life, including your finances.

4. **It is hard to stop obsessing over what was.** Life presents ups and downs, losses and gains. Bad things do happen, and no one is free from the pain of the past or decisions made back then. However, you can focus toward the most precious gift you have—the life God has purposed for you—instead of being immobilized and frozen because of your feelings about the past. You did the best you could with what you knew at the time. Offer yourself a little lovingkindness as you train yourself to take your attention away from your past, one step at a time. One little shift today

will shine a big, bright light on what will happen tomorrow.

5. **You find yourself asking the wrong question.** If you find yourself asking, "Why me?" more often than you ask, "What's next?" then it's definitely time for a change. Don't become a victim of the stories you tell yourself. When something does not turn out as you expected, don't blame someone else or outside circumstances. Through Jesus, you have always had the power to change and to do what needs to be done to produce the results God has destined for you.

   Be willing to ask yourself, "What do I believe?" "What was I thinking?" "How was I feeling?" As you focus on the right questions, the right ideas, and the knowledge that there is always another option, God will always provide the answers.

6. **You have lost your passion.** Your lifestyle no longer fits the person you want to become. Material possessions and money all have their place, but a glorious life can be lived if you are involved in, or actively seeking, something that you are passionate about every day. When you are involved in what you love, you become a person of

interest—someone who is blessed to be a blessing and can inspire someone else.

TRIMMING YOUR SPENDING PLAN

"Why spend money on what is not bread, and your labor on what does not satisfy? Listen, listen to me, and eat what is good, and you will delight in the richest of fare."

Isaiah 55:2, NIV

As you create your spending plan, you will likely need to make some changes to how you use your money by cutting the fat from your spending plan and trimming it down. That may not sound very appealing, but it doesn't mean you have to give up all the things that you love in order to save money. It is possible to change your entire lifestyle for the better by simply adhering to a few budgetary constraints.

Your spending plan consists of fixed expenses and discretionary costs. Fixed expenses include such things as mortgage or rental payments; equity and installment loans; monthly utilities; car, life, and house insurance payments; utility payments such as gas, electric, or water, and payments for services you use like cell phones or cable and satellite TV; school tuition; and child support or alimony payments. Discretionary costs are voluntary expenditures and may increase or decrease as your fixed expenses fluctuate. If your earnings decrease, you'll likely need to reduce discretionary costs first.

Many items are fixed expenses only in that they come out of your paycheck every month or you write checks for them automatically. Yet some can be changed or even renegotiated. Let's look at several in more detail:[4]

Rent or mortgage: Your home is your castle. Yet can you afford the one you currently have? Moving is not something you're going to do tomorrow, but if your rent or mortgage is eating up more than 25 percent of your income, you should plan for a change down the road. See if you can add extra money to your monthly payment to finish off your mortgage faster. Think about moving to a cheaper home or apartment. Tax law provides an incentive to trade down to the tune of $500,000 in tax-free capital gains on a home, no matter your age.

> **It is possible to change your entire lifestyle for the better.**

Utilities: Turn down the heat and air conditioning. Strictly analyze your phone needs. Do you need so many lines? Is your cell phone truly essential?

Insurance: Do an annual check on your life insurance policies, and consider the amount of premiums you are currently paying against the amount of death benefit coverage you have. If the premiums are high and your coverage is low, consider speaking with a life insurance agent about other opportunities that may be available for you. If you currently have a Term Life insurance policy, consider looking at a Whole Life policy, where you have the ability to accumulate tax-deferred wealth. Increase the deductibles on your auto and homeowner policies, too, and drop collision insurance if your car is paid off. Don't skip disability insurance, though. If you can't work, you could jeopardize everything without insurance.

Groceries: Think about the foods that are pleasurable to you. Don't cut corners there. But how about bottled water? Is there really a great difference between the brand for $1.99 and the one for $3.99? Do you really enjoy the frozen or processed foods you buy? Getting the ingredients to make something fresh is often cheaper when you get to the checkout line.

Clothing: The biggest enemy of a clothing spending plan is impulse buying. When you shop, make a list of what you absolutely need and purchase only from your list. Buy the best you can afford and nothing more.

Transportation: This can quickly eat up significant portions of a spending plan. Don't tell yourself you're going to stop visiting your girlfriend or significant other on the weekends, but take a hard look at where you can save. Negotiate for bargain airfares. Cars are better made and last longer than in the past. Get one you like and take good care of it. Keep it for several years. You can also consider walking instead of paying to take a cab or public transportation.

Household and babysitting help: Admittedly, it is tough to cut corners here, but consider it anyway. In the end, if you have found a good caretaker for your children, don't cut their pay or look for someone else.

Credit: Pick up two months' worth of credit card bills and total up the interest you paid. You'll likely be shocked. Paying off your credit cards will provide huge savings.

Taxes: If you are offered one, contribute to your 401(k) at work and make use of health care and dependent care spending accounts. Be careful not to overfund your 401(k), but consider other tax-deferred options for saving money. Remember, diversifying your methods for saving and accumulating passive income can also be a way to build a safe haven of extra cash for unexpected financial setbacks. Be sure to meet with a financial health coach about safe money strategies.

Of course, you must focus on discretionary spending as well. The key, however, is to choose something that enriches your life rather than diminishes it. For example, jot down everything you spend in a notebook. This may seem tedious, but it will be revealing and helpful. Look for the areas where you are needlessly spending and cut it out.

Reviving Your Financial Future

Think of this: every time you forgo a purchase, you can put that same amount of money toward paying off debt or into your savings account. Each time you skip a latte, you have saved at least $3.00. Whenever you decide to walk instead of taking the bus, you have as much as $1.75 for a single one-way trip. At the same time, though, if you use public transportation instead of driving your car, you save on gasoline costs, parking expenses, and the general wear and tear on your automobile. Every time you take your lunch to work instead of buying lunch, you save lots of money, up to $10.00 or more per meal.

Imagine what this could add up to over a 30-day period:

- 30 lattes at $3.00 each = $90
- 30 round-trip bus rides at $3.50 each = $105
- 30 lunches at $10 each = $300

HOW TEMPERAMENTS AND PERSONALITY TYPES IMPACT SPENDING

"For who hath known the mind of the Lord, that he should instruct him? But we have the mind of Christ."

1 Corinthians 2:16, ASV

Financial Healing from the Inside Out

Personality usually refers to the characteristics of a person that is unique and sets them apart from everyone else. Our personalities are what distinguish one person from another. Do a quick Google search of "personality types" and you'll see that psychologists have identified many different variations in our personalities, and that no one single personality type is the ideal one. Much of an individual's personality is shaped by experiences, by societal and cultural influences, by education and career choices, and by family dynamics.

Temperament is one the many facets of our personalities, but temperament and personality are not synonymous. Our temperaments classify us by our emotional attitudes, the foundation for our personalities. It is possible for two individuals to have identical temperaments but be completely different in every other way.

Temperaments are not passing moods or phases in our attitudes. They stay constant throughout our lives from birth until death, even if every other aspect of our personalities change over time.

Gaining an understanding of your individual personality types, as well as those of your loved ones, can be a worthwhile exercise. They are many different personality assessments to help you make that discovery. It's vital because your personality and character traits are directly tied to everything you do, including how you handle your finances.

Reviving Your Financial Future

If you are not aware of which dominant and subordinate personality traits you have, then it's also possible you will not know what it is that you may be wrestling against in terms of disciplining your spending and ability to manage your money.

Understanding why you do what you do plays a great part in positioning yourself to dream and think yourself into financial freedom.

Notes

1. Revive, Resuscitate and Restore! Deborah Waldron Fry. https://www.hiskingdomprophecy.com/revive-resuscitate-and-restore/
2. How to Seek Wise Counsel…Who Should I Talk to? Crystal McDowell. https://www.whatchristianswanttoknow.com/how-to-seek-wise-counselwho-should-i-talk-to/
3. 6 Signs It's Time to Make a Change. Elle Sommer. https://livepurposefullynot.com/6-signs-time-make-change/
4. 10 Ways to Find the Fat in Your Budget. Mary Rowland. http://web.utah.edu/basford/personalfinance/handouts/budgeting/FindFatinBudget.htm

Chapter 5

Dreaming and Thinking Your Way to Financial Freedom

It's been said by many that the most rewarding career and resulting happiness comes when you work in the vocation you would choose if money were not an issue.[1] In other words, if everything financial obligation disappeared tomorrow and you had zero debts, bills, or retirement concerns, what would you decide to do for 40 hours each week? For many, the answer to that question is one of the biggest driving forces behind improving their personal finances.

Yet this happiness seems all too elusive. According to an article published on MoneyManagement.org, seven out of 10 Americans are worried about their personal finances. This is probably connected to the fact that six out of 10 Americans spend without adhering to a spending plan.[2] As a result of this, many people struggle to organize their financial obligations. Several assumptions can be made about those who continue to experience problems with money.

- They are not keeping track of their financial obligations. They do not organize their bills and, therefore, are not sure what needs or doesn't need to be paid. It is possible for some to be so disorganized that they completely forget what they should be paying on a monthly basis.
- They are spending their money on other things. Without implementing a spending plan, there is a good chance that the finances allocated for bill payment will be mistakenly spent on something else. It could be on an unnecessary expense or it could be a payment that doesn't have to be paid yet.
- They lack the knowledge to properly manage their money. The lower their educational attainment, the higher the chance they will fail to pay their bills on time.
- They became too financially confident

and become reckless with their spending. Those who have a seemingly stable financial situation can become complacent, causing them to loosen budgetary restrictions or not pay attention to it at all.

There are some habits you can develop to make the management of your finances easier.

Plan every expenditure. A spending plan, as mentioned in the last chapter, is always a great place to start. It forces you to look into both your income and expenses on a regular basis. You will be in a better position to make decisions when you know your financial capabilities.

Wait before spending. Pause before every expense. This could literally mean leaving the store, going home, and thinking about the expense before purchasing the item you want to buy. This gives you time to consider if the purchase is truly necessary or not. The more expensive the purchase, the more time you should spend thinking about it. This will help you break bad habits such as impulse buying.

Save after every paycheck. Put away the amount you desire to save immediately after getting paid. Even better is to auto debit your savings by transferring it into another account. That way, you will be less prone to spend your savings because it won't be in your checking account.

Minimize debt. If you have existing debt, start paying it off aggressively. If for whatever reason you need to borrow more, make sure your debt level is lower before you add more to it.

Prepare for emergencies. Consider how you can save so you can survive future financial setbacks. Then one unforeseen emergency will not propel you into further debt.

Invest in the future. Finally, learn how to invest for your future. After the Great Recession of December 2007-June 2009, BankofAmerica.com revealed that 40 percent of Americans were reluctant to invest in the stock market—and for some that same hesitance remains today. While it may be scary to risk your money, investing is one of the few ways you can make money work for you to increase your net worth.

WHEN YOU DREAM, DREAM BIGGER

If Jesus were sitting directly in front of you and you could make a single request of Him for whatever your heart desires, what would you ask for? To win the lottery or receive an unexpected financial windfall? For straight A's on the final exam? For better health or help to kick a bad habit? How about a better-paying job, or maybe just any job because you are unemployed or underemployed?

Dreaming and Thinking Your Way to Financial Freedom

Your response will reveal:

- What you value the most.
- Your true priorities.
- Where you actually stand in your relationship with God.

Whatever is in your heart is what you truly believe—and that is what you will take action to achieve. The words of Proverbs provide a vital principle:

"As he thinketh in his heart, so is he"
Proverbs 23:7, KJV

If you believe that you will never be successful or that you can never achieve financial freedom and be debt free, then you will not strive for more than what you currently have and will not make any of the choices necessary to bring yourself to a place to reach financial freedom.

"I think myself happy."
Acts 26:2, KJV

Likewise, we can think small, angry, self-serving thoughts that are cynical, prideful, judging, or greedy—or we can think thoughts of honor, love, graciousness, humility, gratitude, and faith. To "think yourself happy" will require a change of your mindset. It will also necessitate a hunger to improve your life and the lives of others. You will need to see yourself in a better place other than where you are now. You will also need to have faith and believe that what God said is yours is, indeed, yours. Remember, all things are possible with God (Matthew 19:26).

> **Whatever is in your heart is what you truly believe**

Here are seven steps you can take to start dreaming bigger now.

1. **Think positively**. The fastest way to begin doing this is to take your mind off yourself and your problems. Start thinking about how you can help someone else.
2. **Think creatively**. Consider ways to tackle a particular situation differently. Prayerfully begin thinking "outside the box" without placing conditions or limitations on what can be accomplished.
3. **Think purposefully**. Carefully assess all avenues that need to be examined, being mindful of and making preparation for the possibility of encountering challenging situations. In the business world, this is done through a SWOT Analysis, where you list of all your Strengths and Weaknesses (internal factors that show where you

are strong and competitive but may have limited resources) and Opportunities and Threats (external factors that indicate who and where your competitors are and how you may overcome the challenges in dealing with them).

4. **Think elevated thoughts.** This requires moving beyond the chit-chat going on in your head, and utilizing the discernment God has given you to move forward and make decisions without being judgmental, self-sabotaging, or blaming others while expressing confidence in where God is taking you. Consider the majestic eagle. It sits perched high and has a view of the entire area beneath him. The eagle is also a master flyer. It does not needlessly expend its energy by flapping its wings but soars with wings spread wide on currents of strong thermal winds. Finally, the eagle is bold and courageous. It has no fear of engaging the enemy.

5. **Think of solutions to problems that are not necessarily your own.** Listen to and observe a problem while it's in action. It's one thing to read about how an entrepreneur came up with a particular solution; it's quite another to become that entrepreneur yourself. When you can

witness a problem in action, then you can utilize the gifts you already possess to define the moment where a solution is to begin.

6. **Think long-term.** Look beyond the present and ponder ahead about what will happen in the distant future and develop a strategy for sustainability. This does not mean placing something in the back of your mind with the expectation that someday you'll eventually get to it. Rather, you are to actively establish measurable goals with a clear picture in mind, outlining the definitive steps that need to be taken in order to reach each one of those goals, and how long each goal will take to fulfill.

7. **Think possibilities and opportunities.** Possibilities are *everything* that the enemy tried to make you believe was impossible. Opportunities are *all* the blessings and open doors God has made available for you to walk through as you are abide in Him.

HOW WILL YOU KNOW WHEN MONEY IS NO LONGER AN ISSUE?

It happens when you can make a clear distinction can be made between your needs and your wants.[3]

Dreaming and Thinking Your Way to Financial Freedom

The distinction between a need and a want is quite simple, at least on the surface:

- A need is something you have to have.
- A want is something you would like to have.

In actuality, there are only four things that you must *have* in order to survive:

1. Shelter: a roof over your head to provide protection from the elements.
2. Food and water: to maintain your physical health.
3. Clothing: to remain comfortable and be appropriately dressed.
4. Basic health care and hygiene products.

Everything else beyond this—a big house, name-brand clothes and shoes, fancy foods and drinks, a brand new car—are considered to be a want.

Nearly everyone would like to be able to earn or make more money, and there is nothing wrong with trying to achieve more. However, it's important to understand what is behind your drive to get more. You may *think* that you have to make more—and you may be right. But you could find that your situation is more solid that you had realized.

How do you know when money is no longer an issue?

You have no consumer debt. Debt is a four-letter word in more ways than one. Some debt may be okay, but it is usually a warning sign that you are in financial peril. If you are debt-free, chances are high you are earning enough money.

Growing savings. If you notice that your savings balance is the same or somewhat higher at the end of the month than at the beginning, then you are doing something right. Namely, you are living within your means. That's a strong signal that your income is sufficient.

Autopay bills. If you have to "borrow from Peter in order to pay Paul" each month, then you probably won't be able to put your bills on automatic payment. But if you are able to put all your bills on autopay without worrying about being overdrawn, you are doing fine and don't need to worry about earning more.

You are spending more. If you notice that you are spending a little more this year than last and haven't gone into debt or invaded your savings or investments to do so, it's a good sign that you are earning enough money.

You never find yourself saying, "If only I had more money, I could…" If you are living the life you want and are able to achieve the things that are really important to you, money is no longer a problem.

Helping others. The number one sign that you earn enough is that you help others willingly and generously. This includes going the extra mile for people you care about (when appropriate) and, of course, giving to your church and to charities.

As you can see, money not being an issue and being able to earn enough is all relative. "Enough" for you may not be nearly enough for your neighbor. But just because you may earn enough now doesn't mean that you should sit back and let life roll by. Revisit your financial plan regularly, at least on an annual basis. If things are exactly as you want them, enjoy. But if there is the possibility of retiring earlier, or helping other people in a greater way, then it might make sense to amend your spending plan and make changes to your savings and investment strategy.

THE FREEDOM CHALLENGE

Financial freedom may look different for each person, but freedom from finances generally means being free of all debt: no outstanding loans, no credit card debt (never carrying any balances forward and incurring added interest), and no mortgages. It means no payments to anyone for any reason.

Financial freedom can also mean that you now have multiple revenue streams—savings and investments that allow enough flexibility for you to be able to retire to do what you want when you want and how often you want, where you choose to do it for however long you want to do it. Financial freedom is being able to enjoy a self-directed life where you get to call all the shots in terms of how, when, and where you spend your time. Financial freedom may also be the choice of living a frugal lifestyle rather than acting in an irresponsible manner, especially if failure to do so will put your financial freedom at risk.

> **True financial freedom shows that you have taken control of your finances.**

True financial freedom shows that you have taken control of your finances. It's just you and God, and you will do whatever He instructs you to do with what He has birthed in and through you. You are not dependent on anyone else, and no one else dictates how to spend your money.

There are six stages to financial freedom:[4]

Stage 1 – Solvency

This is where you can meet your financial commitments, your income exceeds your expenses, and you are no longer accumulating debt.

Stage 2 – Stability

At this stage, you have repaid your consumer debt, established emergency savings, and continue to earn a personal profit. You may still have college loans and a mortgage, but you have eliminated other obligations and have built a buffer of savings to protect yourself from unfortunate events.

Stage 3 – Agency

You work and live how and where you want. You have eliminated all debt including student loans and mortgages. You now have enough money that you could quit your job at a moment's notice without hesitation.

Stage 4 – Security

This is where your investment income can cover your basic needs. Even if you never work another day in your life, you have enough to afford simple housing, basic food, essential clothing, and insurance.

Stage 5 – Independence

At this stage, your investment income is sufficient to fund your current standard of living for the remainder of your life. You can afford the basics, but you can also afford some comforts as well.

Stage 6 – Abundance

At this final stage, you have "enough, and then some." Your passive income from all sources will not only fund your lifestyle indefinitely, but it will grant you the freedom to do whatever you want to do. You can share your wealth with others, explore the world, or even build an empire.

"I'M FREE! I'M FREE! THANK GOD, I'M FREE!"

"What then shall we then say to these things? If God is for us, who can be against us? ... Yet in all these things we are more than conquerors through Him who loved us. For I am persuaded that neither death nor life, nor angels not principalities nor powers, nor things present nor things to come, nor height nor depth, nor any other created thing, shall be able to separate us from the love of God which is in Christ Jesus our Lord."

Romans 8:31, 37-39, NKJV

Now, declare the Word of God for your life right now!

What then shall we say to these things? [financial things]

If God is for us [financially]***, who can be against us?*** [financially]

For I am persuaded [convinced that we are wealth magnets and that we have the wealth of the one percent]

[and knowing these things] ***We are more than conquerors.***

[and I am convinced that no matter what goes on, be it death or life to my finances] ***that neither death nor life, nor angels nor principalities nor powers, nor things***

> ***present nor things to come, nor height nor depth, nor any other created thing,***
>
> ***shall be able to separate us*** [to use our finances/His financial wealth through us to do the things He has required for His Kingdom]
>
> ***from the love of God which is in Christ Jesus our Lord.***

Take a moment to pause and commit yourself to these words. God will bless you and enrich you because you already know you are victorious. You are not a victim. You may have been up and down in the past, but you are now steady because you know that God is *with* you and you are assured of what He has prepared *for* you.

You have to envision it and see it, and then you have to say it. Speak it over your life daily. Declare that you will have everything God has promised you. Look in the mirror and speak freedom to yourself. In all aspects of your life, Christ has given you victory. You also have victory in the financial realm. You have it because your mind has now changed the way it thinks since God has revealed Himself to you in such a mighty way.

You are now His ambassador in this earth realm.

You are no longer *employed* by the world system. You are *deployed* by the Kingdom.

You're free! You're free! Thank God, you're free!

Notes

1. What would you do with your life if money were not an issue? G.E. Miller. https://20somethingfinance.com/what-would-you-do-if-money-were-not-an-issue/
2. Money Management is a Top Financial Issue for Americans. National Debt Relief. https://www.nationaldebtrelief.com/money-management-top-financial-issue-americans/
3. Distinguishing Between Wants and Needs. Erin Huffstetler. https://www.thebalance.com/wants-vs-needs-1388544
4. The stages of financial freedom: The road to financial independence. J.D. Roth. https://www.getrichslowly.org/stages-of-financial-freedom/

Your Personal Notes

Your Personal Notes

Your Personal Notes

Your Personal Notes

Your Personal Notes

Your Personal Notes

Your Personal Notes

Your Personal Notes

Your Personal Notes

Your Personal Notes

About the Authors

Angela C. Preston is driven by the belief that "success begins with a passion, a dream, a plan, a system, and a made-up mind." Her mission is to empower individuals and families to secure their financial futures. As the Owner and President of Diamond Elite Loan Signing Institute, she is committed to transforming notaries into Loan Signing Agents and assisting individuals in creating comprehensive wealth management systems that cater to diverse lifestyles through capital management and infinite banking strategies.

Angela graduated summa cum laude with a Bachelor of Science in Finance from Regis University in Denver, Colorado. She is also a certified financial health coach and credit counselor, affiliated with the National Association of Credit Counselors. As a licensed minister, Angela uniquely merges her spiritual focus with financial education by traveling across the country to teach transformative principles of personal financial freedom, integrating biblical insights with solid financial strategies.

With over 28 years of experience in the Denver area, Angela is passionate about coaching, mentoring, teaching, and motivating others. Reach Angela at:

> Aototally@comcast.com or
> @diamondeliteloansigning

About the Authors

Dr. Amanda H. Goodson is the President and CEO of Amanda Goodson Global, LLC, where she provides executive leadership coaching, speaking engagements, and training. Additionally, she heads Never the Same Arizona, a 501(c)(3) organization focused on financial wellness. Amanda is an Amazon Best-Selling Author and has penned over 30 books.

Her knowledge, infectious energy, interactive techniques, and insightful intellect stem from more than 25 years of experience in leading and managing diverse teams and complex systems. As a speaker, coach, or trainer, Amanda is poised to inspire and motivate you with her expertise in goal setting and achievement strategies. She will leverage her insights from her remarkable journey from meager beginnings to being the first African American woman appointed as Director of Safety & Mission Assurance at NASA, serving as an innovative executive director at a prominent engineering firm, and engaging as an independent certified John Maxwell leadership coach, educator, and speaker.

Reach Amanda at amandagoodsonglobal@gmail.com, amandagoodson.com, or neverthesameaz.org.

www.ingramcontent.com/pod-product-compliance
Lightning Source LLC
Chambersburg PA
CBHW021447210526
45463CB00002B/662